ANIMAL CROSSING:
Gathering and Crafting

CHERRY LAKE PUBLISHING • ANN ARBOR, MICHIGAN

by Josh Gregory

T0027063

CHERRY LAKE PRESS

Published in the United States of America by Cherry Lake Publishing
Ann Arbor, Michigan
www.cherrylakepublishing.com

Reading Adviser: Beth Walker Gambro, MS, Ed., Reading Consultant, Yorkville, IL

Cherry Lake Press is an imprint of Cherry Lake Publishing Group

Library of Congress Cataloging-in-Publication Data has been filed and is available
at catalog.loc.gov

Cherry Lake Publishing Group would like to acknowledge the work of the
Partnership for 21st Century Learning, a Network of Battelle for Kids. Please
visit http://www.batelleforkids.org/networks/p21 for more information.

Printed in the United States of America
Corporate Graphics

Contents

Chapter 1

Tools of the Trade

Animal Crossing: New Horizons is a game that is all about building your own world. After traveling to a deserted island, you are left to explore it and build it up however you want. The island is jam-packed with all the resources you need to create a cozy home. You can construct homes and businesses and encourage new characters to move in. You can also collect supplies from the island and use them to **craft** everything from simple furniture to strange

Keep crafting!

All done for now.

I made a
flimsy watering can!

Flimsy tools will likely be some of the items you craft most often as you play *Animal Crossing: New Horizons*.

decorations. With enough effort, you can turn the empty island into a bustling town that is completely unique to you. No two players will have islands that are exactly the same!

You'll be empty-handed when you first reach your new island home. Luckily, a few characters will join you on the journey. They will give you the first tools and tips you need to get started exploring and gathering the supplies you need to build you new home. Tom Nook is one of the major characters in the game. If you keep talking to him and doing as he asks, he will introduce you to a lot of the game's basics. He will also give you your first few DIY (do-it-yourself) recipes. Each recipe allows you to craft a new item. The first recipes you get will be for some basic tools. These tools are incredibly important. They will allow you to explore new parts of the island and collect the ingredients you need to craft all kinds of other things.

Very early on, Tom will give you recipes for the flimsy axe, flimsy watering can, flimsy bug net, and flimsy fishing rod. These basic tools will open up a lot of possibilities for your island adventures. Axes are used to chop trees. Your watering can will help you grow flowers and other plants. A bug net lets you catch bugs, while a fishing rod lets you catch fish. All of these activities play an important role in developing your island, so take some time to get used to the way each tool works.

If you keep working for Tom Nook, he will soon invite a friend named Blathers to the island. Blathers will give you another important new tool recipe: the

Watering your existing flowers will allow new ones to grow nearby. Sometimes the new ones will have unexpected colors!

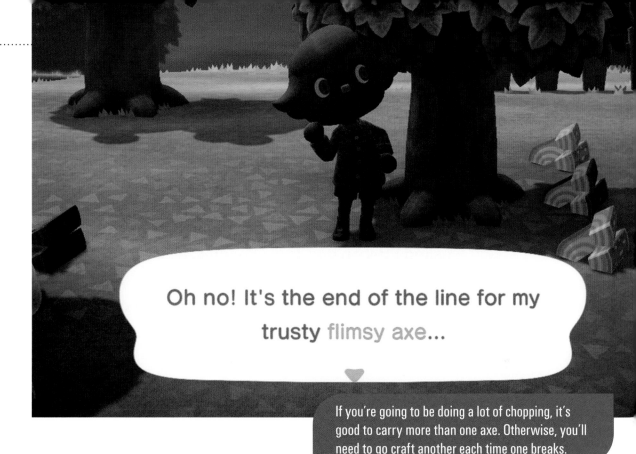

Oh no! It's the end of the line for my trusty flimsy axe...

If you're going to be doing a lot of chopping, it's good to carry more than one axe. Otherwise, you'll need to go craft another each time one breaks.

flimsy shovel. This tool has several uses. Of course, it can be used to dig holes. This will let you find things buried underground. It also allows you to bury things yourself and uproot tree stumps.

Each tool you get has a certain amount of **durability**. Once you use it enough times, a tool will break and disappear from your **inventory**. Your flimsy tools will only last for a few uses each before you need to replace them. You could find yourself going through supplies very quickly as you craft replacements for your broken tools. Luckily, it's pretty easy to earn DIY recipes for upgraded versions of all the flimsy tools. All you need to do is visit the Nook Stop computer in the Resident Services building. Here, you can use Nook Miles to purchase an item called Pretty Good Tools Recipes. This will allow you to craft better versions of the axe, shovel, watering can, bug net, and fishing rod. For each one, you'll need to start with the flimsy version of the tool. Then you'll need

Unlike the flimsy axe, the upgraded version has a sharp metal blade.

Switching It Up

Are you getting tired of how long it takes to switch from one tool to another? Head to the Nook Stop and trade some Nook Miles for an item called Tool Ring: It's Essential. This will unlock a new feature called the tool ring. Press the up arrow button to bring up a ring showing all of the tools currently in your inventory. Then use the left stick to choose which tool you want to use. This makes it possible to quickly swap one tool for another instead of cycling through them to find the one you need. It's a very handy feature that will save you a lot of hassle as you play.

to add materials such as wood or iron. This will give you more durable versions of your tools.

Want even better versions of your tools? You'll have to work hard and spend a lot of time tending to your island. There are DIY recipes for special golden versions of each of the tools. Each one of these recipes is a reward for completing one of the game's major goals. For example, catching every bug **species** in the game will give you the recipe for the golden bug net. Catching every fish will earn you the ability to craft a golden fishing rod. You'll get the golden axe recipe after breaking 100 other axes. The golden shovel comes from helping a character named Gulliver at least 30 times. The golden watering can comes from earning a five-star rating. Golden tools are expensive to craft, but they last a very long time. They still don't last forever, though. You'll need to craft them all over again if they break!

If you don't feel like crafting flimsy tools, you can also buy them from Timmy and Tommy at the Nook's Cranny shop. If you help the twins upgrade to a larger shop, they will also start stocking a variety of special tools that can't be crafted at all. For example, you can find a watering can shaped like an elephant and a more colorful fishing rod. These tools all have the same

Until you are quite far along in the game, large portions of your island can only be reached using a ladder.

durability as the versions you can craft after getting the Pretty Good Tools Recipes. They simply have different looks.

You'll also get a couple of important tools that help you travel around obstacles on the island. Blathers gives you a recipe for the vaulting pole at the same time as the one for the flimsy shovel. This pole will let you jump across rivers, even when there are no bridges nearby. After you've built up your island a bit and helped Tom Nook bring in new villagers, you'll also get a recipe for a ladder. This handy item lets you climb up to the high cliffs on your island. Certain items can only be found up high, so this is extremely useful.

Unlike most of your tools, the vaulting pole and ladder cannot break. This ensures that you can't get trapped on part of the island with no way to get back to a crafting table. It also means there is no need to upgrade them. Once you have these useful tools in your inventory, it's best to simply keep them there all the time. In fact, it's a good idea to keep at least one of each tool on you all the time. After all, you never know when you might need to dig, chop, or catch something.

Chapter 2

Stocking Up on Supplies

E ach crafting recipe has a list of ingredients that you'll need to craft it. All of these ingredients can be found on your island or crafted. It's simply a matter of finding and collecting everything you'll need.

Perhaps the easiest crafting materials to get are clumps of weeds. These simply appear on the ground all over the island. All you need to do is pick them up.

Need more weeds? Simply leave your island alone for a few days. When you return, there will be plenty to pick!

If a tree has fruit growing on it, the fruit will all fall off when you shake it.

There will be a lot of them when you first reach the island, and more will continue to pop up every day.

The trees on your island are one of your main sources of crafting materials. As you walk around, you will probably notice branches lying all over the ground. If you need more, you can also walk up to any tree and press the A button to shake it. All kinds of things can drop out of trees when you shake them. Sometimes you will even get bags of money or random pieces of furniture. If you're unlucky, you might disturb a wasp nest. (Once you get away from the angry wasps, you can pick up the nest and use it for crafting!) Among all those other things, tree branches will also fall. Simply keep shaking any tree and more branches will keep falling. This means you have an unlimited supply of this material as long as you have access to trees.

Trees can also be chopped using an axe. This will produce three very important crafting items: wood, softwood, and hardwood. Each tree on your island can give you three of these materials per day. Which ones you get is random. Be careful which axe you use

Avoid picking up wood until you've chopped all the trees you want to for the day. That way, you can see which ones you already chopped!

when chopping trees. The flimsy axe or stone axe can produce wood without damaging a tree. But if you use the regular axe or golden axe, you will chop the tree down on the third hit. This is useful if you want to get rid of a tree. But you definitely don't want to clear all the trees from your island at once. In fact, it is very useful to plant extra trees as soon as you can. You can do this by purchasing saplings from Nook's Cranny. Use your shovel to dig a hole, then plant the sapling. It will soon grow into a resource-packed tree. If you want more fruit trees, simply plant pieces of fruit in the ground.

You might also notice large rocks as you wander the island. These are also an important source of crafting materials. When you hit a rock with a shovel or an axe, it will drop one of several items. Clay and stone are the most common. Iron nuggets are slightly rarer, and gold nuggets are very rare. All of these are used in crafting recipes.

Each rock on your island can drop up to eight materials each day. However, there is a trick to getting the most out of your rocks. After you hit a rock the first time, you have a very short window of time to keep

Distant Lands

Looking to stock up on supplies without chopping down all of your trees or busting up all of your rocks? Spend some Nook Miles at the Nook Stop to buy an item called a Nook Miles Ticket. Then head to the airport on the southern coast of the island. Here, you can trade your Nook Miles Ticket for a trip to a small mystery island.

You never know exactly what you will find on these islands, but they almost always have a variety of plants and other useful resources. Grab everything you want. Chop down every tree and break every rock. You can never come back to the same island twice, so there is no reason to worry about wrecking it. Go wild and fill up your pockets with supplies. Then buy another Nook Miles Ticket and do it again!

hitting it before it stops dropping items. To make things even tougher, you will be bounced backward each time you hit the rock. This slows you down from hitting it over and over again. The simple way around this is to dig a hole behind your character before you start hitting the rock. The hole will block your character from moving backward with each hit. This will let you get the full eight hits before the rock stops dropping items!

At any point, there can be up to six rocks on your island. Their locations are random. However, you can make them change locations by destroying them. First, eat a piece of fruit. This will give you extra strength. Then smack a rock with a shovel or a stone axe. This will break the rock apart. The next day, a new one will show up in a different location. You don't get to choose the location, though.

One crafting item you won't find on your island at first is bamboo. To get this, you'll first need to visit a mystery island where it happens to grow. Use a shovel to dig up a bamboo shoot, then bring it to your home island and plant it. The bamboo shoot will grow into a bamboo tree. After that, you can hit the tree with your

Simply dig holes like this before hitting a rock to avoid getting knocked backward.

axe to get bamboo pieces, just like you get wood from regular trees.

Some recipes require fruit or flowers. Only certain types of fruit and flowers are **native** to your island. To get others, you'll need to travel to mystery islands or visit your friends. Then you can bring back fruit and flowers from those islands to plant on yours. Eventually, you can have every type of plant growing on your island. This will take some time, though!

During certain times of the year, you'll be able to find special seasonal crafting items. For example, you can use your net to snag cherry blossom petals

You can use your net to swipe snowflakes from the sky during winter. Somehow, they won't melt if you leave them in your pockets all year long!

in spring and snowflakes in winter. Or you can find colorful eggs all around the island around the time of the spring Bunny Day holiday. These seasonal items are often tied to special activities. Characters on the island will often give you special DIY recipes that make use of seasonal materials. They might also challenge you to craft certain items by a certain date. Talk to everyone and see what happens!

At night, you might be lucky enough to witness a meteor shower in the sky above your island. These events aren't just for show. They are also a way to get special rare crafting materials. When you see shooting stars in the sky, press up on the right stick to look upward. Press the A button as a star jets across the sky and you will make a wish. You can do this multiple times if there are a lot of shooting stars in the sky that night. The next day, you will find star fragments on your beaches. There are different kinds, and which ones you get depends on the date. This is the only way to get star fragments, so don't miss out.

Chapter 3

Recipes for Success

By now, your pockets are probably bursting with crafting supplies. So what can you do with them? Start crafting things, of course!

To craft, you'll need a workbench. At the start of the game, Tom Nook will have one you can use in his tent. Later on, there will be one in the Resident Services building. However, you can also craft more workbenches and put them wherever you want. There

A workbench is an essential item in any *Animal Crossing* home.

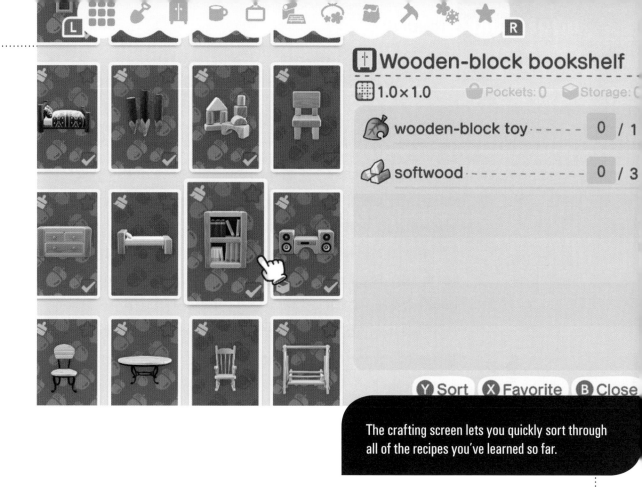

The crafting screen lets you quickly sort through all of the recipes you've learned so far.

are all kinds of different workbench designs. Even though they all look different, there is no difference in how they work.

Approach a workbench and press the A button to get started. You will then see a list of all the DIY recipes you have so far. Pressing the L or R buttons lets you scroll through different categories of recipes. Select a recipe and press the A button to take a closer look. Now you will get a list of the materials needed to craft the item. You can also see how much space the item will take up in a room and how many you currently own. The game will also let you know if it is something you have crafted before.

If you have the necessary materials in your inventory, all you need to do is choose "Craft it!" to get started. Your character will get to work, and the newly crafted item will show up right away in your inventory. Keep in mind that crafting materials must be in your inventory before you use the workbench. Materials that are lying on the ground or stored elsewhere cannot be used to craft.

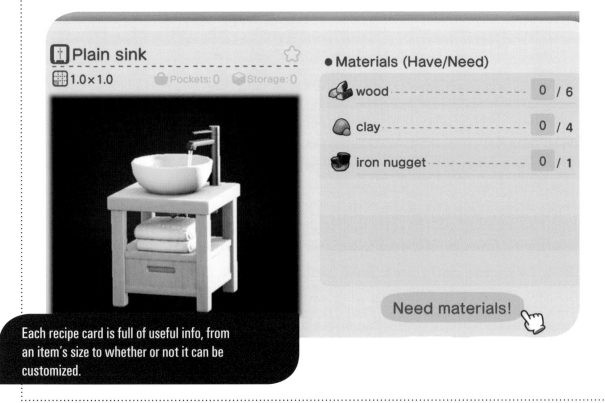

Plain sink

1.0×1.0   Pockets: 0   Storage: 0

● Materials (Have/Need)

wood - - - - - - - - - - - - - - - - 0 / 6

clay - - - - - - - - - - - - - - - - 0 / 4

iron nugget - - - - - - - - - - - 0 / 1

Need materials!

Each recipe card is full of useful info, from an item's size to whether or not it can be customized.

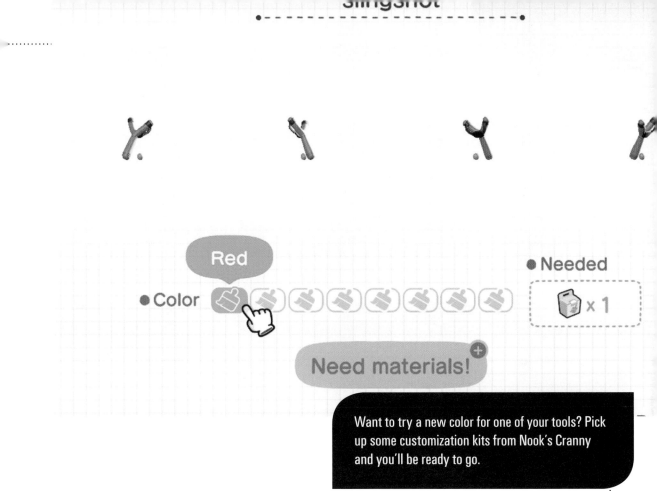

● Color   Red

● Needed   x 1

Need materials!

Want to try a new color for one of your tools? Pick up some customization kits from Nook's Cranny and you'll be ready to go.

Some crafting items can also be customized. A recipe card will be marked with a little paintbrush icon if it is possible to customize the item. Customization usually lets you change an item's color or other things about its appearance. First, you'll need to craft the item. Then you can choose to customize it. Each time you customize something, you need to use a customization kit. These kits can be purchased from Nook's Cranny. Like crafting materials, you'll need them in your inventory when you are ready to customize something.

There are hundreds of different DIY recipes to find in *Animal Crossing: New Horizons*. You'll get a few basic ones to start you out when you complete Tom Nook's requests. But after that, it's up to you to hunt down new recipes. The easiest ones to find are in recipe books you can purchase at Nook's Cranny. Others will be given to you automatically when you do certain things for the first time. For example, the first time you dig up a manila clam on the beach, you will get a recipe to turn clams into fish bait.

Each day, you should take a walk along the beach and look for message bottles. You should be able to find one or two of these each day. Each bottle contains a new DIY recipe, so it's worth hunting them down. You can also find DIY recipes inside the presents that occasionally float through the sky attached to balloons. You should be able to find one of these every few minutes. When you do, get out a slingshot. (You can buy a slingshot or a slingshot DIY recipe from Nook's Cranny.) Then take aim and shoot the balloon. The present will fall down for you to collect. It could have anything from furniture to a recipe inside.

Sometimes your fellow villagers will also give you recipes if you talk to them. Try visiting them when

Running Out of Room

As you start gathering supplies and crafting things, you'll soon run out of space in your inventory to hold everything. There are several things you can do when this happens. First of all, you can simply drop things on the ground. Items will stay wherever you leave them until you pick them up again. You might not want a bunch of junk lying around the island, though. One way to solve this is to expand the size of your inventory. Visit the Nook Stop and purchase the Pocket Organization Guide. This will give you 10 more slots to store items in your pockets. A few days later, another item called Ultimate Pocket Stuffing will show up for sale through Nook Stop. Buy that one to get another 10 inventory slots.

You can also store items at your house. Press the right arrow button to access your home storage any time you are in the house. At first, you'll have 80 storage slots to work with. But you will get more each time you pay Tom Nook to upgrade your house. The total for a fully upgraded house is 2,400 spaces! That should be more than enough to store all of your valuables.

they are at home. You might catch them hard at work at their own workbenches. If you talk to them when this happens, they will teach you the project they are crafting.

After a while, you might start finding cards for DIY recipes you already know. Hang on to these and trade them with your friends. The recipes each player finds are random. You never know who might have a spare card for the recipe you want.

Chapter 4

Cold Hard Cash

Crafting is great for getting all the interesting items you need to decorate your house and island. It's also a great way of making money. All you need to do is craft items and take them to Nook's Cranny. Timmy and Tommy will buy anything you make. They always offer a fair price, so it's always worth it to sell things you don't need.

The best way to make money fast is to ask Timmy and Tommy what's hot. They will tell you an item they

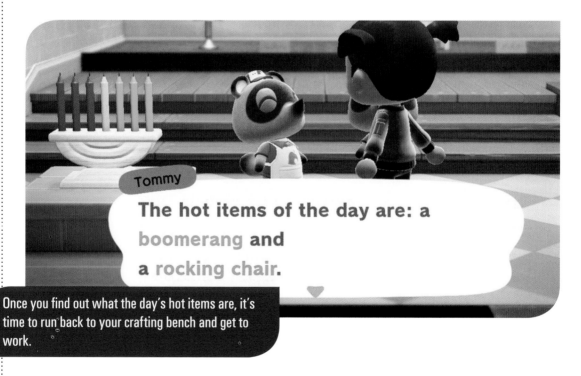

Tommy

The hot items of the day are: a boomerang and a rocking chair.

Once you find out what the day's hot items are, it's time to run back to your crafting bench and get to work.

Yeah, let's sell!

How does this work?

Nah, not now.

It's the store's drop-off box.
Should I sell something?

There is a box outside Nook's Cranny where you can drop things to be sold even if the shop is closed. The downside is that you won't get the full price for your items.

are currently paying double the normal price for. If you have the recipe for this item, you can craft as many as you like and sell them for a huge **profit**. The hot item changes each day, so be sure to check in each time you play.

Crafting materials can also be sold directly to Timmy and Tommy if you need cash fast. For example, gold nuggets can be sold for 10,000 Bells each. However, you will almost always get more money if you take the time to craft something instead of just selling resources.

Have you accidentally sold furniture or clothing you want back, but you don't have the resources or recipe to craft it? Don't worry. All you need to do is visit the Nook Stop and choose "Nook Shopping." Then select one of the catalog icons at the bottom of the screen. This will give you a list of all the items you

Everything

L   R

56,680

Backyard-fence wall

Backyard lawn   Not for sale

Bell-bag rug   Not for sale

Black two-toned tile wall   1,850

Black wooden-deck rug   1,500

Blue desert-tile flooring   2,100

Blue-design kitchen mat   1,000

Blue playroom wall   2,540

Brachio pelvis   Not for sale

Brachio skull   Not for sale

Did you get rid of the perfect flooring for your new decorating plan? You can always buy it again from the catalog.

Miles and Miles

Not everything in *Animal Crossing* can be purchased using Bells. There is also another form of **currency** called Nook Miles. Check out the Nook Miles+ app on your NookPhone. There are all kinds of goals listed that will each earn you miles. Many of these goals revolve around gathering and crafting. You'll complete them naturally as you play. But if you need miles in a hurry, make a point of trying to complete tasks as quickly as you can!

have ever owned, even if you have sold them or traded them to friends. You'll have to pay some Bells, but you can get your items back. You can also use this feature to get multiple copies of an item if you want. Items you purchase will be mailed to you the next day.

With a little luck and some effort, you can craft the island of your dreams. Are you ready to start exploring and experimenting? What will you craft next?

Glossary

craft (KRAFT) make or build something

currency (KUR-uhn-see) a system of money

durability (dur-uh-BIL-uh-tee) a measurement of how much something can be used before it starts to break

inventory (IN-vuhn-toh-ree) a list of the items your character is carrying in a video game

native (NAY-tiv) found naturally in a certain place

profit (PRAH-fit) the amount of money gained from a job or investment

species (SPEE-sheez) a particular category of animals or other living things

Find Out More

BOOKS

Cunningham, Kevin. *Video Game Designer*. Ann Arbor, MI: Cherry Lake Publishing, 2016.

Loh-Hagan, Virginia. *Video Games*. Ann Arbor, MI: Cherry Lake Publishing, 2021.

Powell, Marie. *Asking Questions About Video Games*. Ann Arbor, MI: Cherry Lake Publishing, 2016.

WEBSITES

Animal Crossing Wiki
https://animalcrossing.fandom.com/wiki/Animal_Crossing: _New_Horizons
This fan-created site is packed with info about every detail of the *Animal Crossing* games.

Island News — *Animal Crossing: New Horizons*
https://www.animal-crossing.com/new-horizons/news
Keep up to date with the latest official news updates about *Animal Crossing*.

Index

About the Author

Josh Gregory is the author of more than 150 books for kids. He has written about everything from animals to technology to history. A graduate of the University of Missouri–Columbia, he currently lives in Chicago, Illinois.